HOW TO BE AN

Old Person

*EVERYTHING TO KNOW FOR THE
NEWLY OLD, RETIRING, ELDERLY,
OR CONSIDERING*

By Brian Boone
Leading Oldologist

HUMORIST
BOOKS

New York

First Edition: 2021

ISBN: 978-1-954158-09-2

Humorist Books is an imprint of *Weekly Humorist* owned and operated by Humorist Media LLC.

Weekly Humorist is a weekly humor publication, subscribe online at
weeklyhumorist.com
110 Wall Street New York, NY 10005
weeklyhumorist.com - humoristbooks.com - humoristmedia.com

Design and illustrations by Marty Dundics
Edited by Andy Newton

Thank you to my parents, who are the inspiration for this book, having unabashedly and amusingly behaved like Old People since they were in their early forties.

TABLE OF CONTENTS

The Good Old Days Are the New Old Days!

THE GOOD OLD DAYS ARE THE NEW OLD DAYS!

Greetings, Old Person.

As one of the world's most celebrated and pioneering oldologists, I've long studied Old Persons and their quirks — why they do what they do, say what they say, act how they act, eat what they eat, and smell how they smell. It's a calling I take very seriously, and as the director of the Center of Oldological Technologies (C.O.O.T.), founded with a generous grant from the Department of Aging (D.O.A.), I'm blessed to follow my intellectual passion and oversee a team of world-class oldologists.

And yet, I never thought about writing a book about what it feels like to be an Old Person — or, more accurately, how to move into life as a newly old Old Person. That's all thanks to a chance encounter. One night after work, I stopped at a grocery store to grab a couple of things. I craved a candy bar, and as I stood there, trying to select a treat, a male subject of about 80 years of age ambled up with his walker and planted himself between me and the candy. He stood there for 10 minutes, while he carefully contemplated his options. Whistling throughout (except for the occasional wet coughing fit), he chose a bag of Werther's Originals and was on his way, tipping his Marines cap to me as he departed.

I found the encounter to be both captivating and exhilarating. Here, I had found the very quintessence of the Old Person. He was rude, entitled, made use of a mobility-enabling device, wore a hat, and loved hard candy. I went home right away and feverishly started working on a book to help Old Persons both navigate and embrace their Old Personness, just like the stranger in the store. For an emerging Old Person, all of life can feel like they're in a record store, or a medical clinic with more than two doors: scary and confusing. So here then is this guide for brand-new Old Persons, a thorough catalog of what they can expect when they're disintegrating.

I hope this guide is helpful to you, and please send in all your letters full of complaints handwritten in cursive.

—Brian Boone, Oldologist, PhD, CPA

Chapter One
Start Being an Old Person Right Now!

We know you're champing at the bit to get started on being an Old Person. But hold your horses! You'll get there. You just first need to learn the basics of Old Personness.

How to Be an Old Person
The Official Checklist

To ensure your status as an Old Person, make sure you do all of these vital Old Person things at least once *every* day, and *every* five minutes!

- ☐ Whistle a little tune

- ☐ Hum a little ditty

- ☐ Wink at a stranger

- ☐ Tip your hat (men only)

- ☐ Nod politely to a passerby (women only)

- ☐ Hitch up your pants (men only)

- ☐ Yawn and say, "Oh my!" (women only)

- ☐ Chew on a toothpick

- ☐ Clear your throat

- ☐ Cough apocalyptically

- ☐ Talk to yourself

- ☐ Say "Huh?" and cup your hand over your ear

- ☐ Make bones audibly ache

- ☐ Say, "Oh, these old bones of mine!"

- ☐ Lick your lips

- ☐ Wipe away the weird white stuff off that gathers at the corner of your mouth

- ☐ Clean your glasses with your hot breath

- ☐ Fiddle around in your ear with your finger

- ☐ Fiddle around with the change in your pocket

- ☐ Comment on the weather

- ☐ Ask to speak to the manager

- ☐ Flirt with a waitress or bagboy

- ☐ Complain about "all that racket"

- ☐ Urinate with at least a moderate amount of difficulty

- ☐ Urinate so freely, you don't even realize you're urinating

- ☐ Grumble

PICKING YOUR NEW OLD PERSON NAME

When you become an Old Person, you get to pick a new name — just like the pope, or a king or queen! You'll need one that's suitably Old Person-y, so select one of the following…and *only* one of the following.

LADIES:	GENTLEMEN:
Pearl	Bob
Rose	Gene
Agnes	Ralph
Clara	Harry
Florence	Larry
Gladys	Arthur
Mavis	Lewis
Virginia	Fred
Marie	Walter
Edith	Harvey
Ethel	Dick
Esther	Gus
Dolores	Hugh
Opal	Chester
Hazel	Albert
Iris	Frank
Evelyn	Bud
Beatrice	Abraham
Mabel	Chester
Vera	Gordon
Eunice	Cornelius
Frances	Lloyd
Estelle	Sidney
Ruth	Stanley
Louise	Vernon
Peggy	Harvey

"Guess Who Died?"

Extra! Extra! Ha-ha, just kidding! That's what the old-timey newsboys say when they're selling a newspaper hot off the presses detailing vital, breaking news from several hours earlier. You'll feel like a newsboy, or an intrepid and daring reporter in a "press" hat or even a handsome local TV news anchor fulfilling your duty, because, as an Old Person, you are the bearer of important, vital, and up-to-date news. Specifically, it is up to you to share, spread, and break the news of who died. Well, not everyone or all the time. You just have to keep track of, and then share, the news of what fellow Old Persons in your social circle of fellow Old Persons have kicked the proverbial bucket.

It's a fact of life for an Old Person that death lurks constantly. You're an Old Person, so all of your friends are also Old Persons, and Old Persons tend to die with alarming regularity. Because everybody lives so far apart these days and doesn't chit-chat on the phone to each other every day for an hour or two like they should, the news of an Old Person dying may take days or even weeks to fully spread. It's your job as an Old Person to tell everyone you meet about an Old Person who died, whether they knew that person very well or not. A good way to broach the subject is to walk up to someone you at least think you know and say, "Guess who died?" or "Did you hear who died?" And then you say the name of the person who died, and then you say that "it's such a shame."

Some reporting tips:

• Did that lady across the street with the little dog die? You better tell your adult children, who never met the women, or her dog. But they like dogs, and they know you have a neighbor.

• That movie star you liked, the one who was in the musical in 1950 (*see,* **The Glamorous World of Movie Stars**), died. It's such a shame that he died. Better tell the next person you see on the street during your morning stroll.

• Did your husband's work associate from 20 years ago meet his maker? It's important you tell your church friends who didn't meet him and never even heard you or your long-dead husband even so much as mention them, so they can live every moment of their lives to its fullest.

The Old Person Money Philosophy

Even though you've spent a good six, seven, eight, or more decades on this planet, going through the motions of daily life — and under the absolutely perfect and robust systems of capitalism specifically and especially — working for years at a single, 30-year job you didn't really like or ever want to do but steadfastly and nobly held on to so as to provide for your spouse and children, trading your hard-earned income for goods and services literally thousands of times, you're an Old Person now. This means you instantly and completely lost all understanding of how money works.

To wit: Everything is really expensive to you, but also, somehow, all items are very, very cheap.

For example, you will balk at buying most anything on account of how you get by on a "fixed income," as a retiree living off of a pension, savings, or Social Security. That isn't *really* a fixed income — you're getting free money and health care, which costs everybody else a lot of money. Nevertheless, you will complain about how things cost more than they used to and rail against this fact, as if you're unfamiliar with the notion of inflation. Even worse, you'll protest this broad and immovable economic force by trying to haggle down prices at the grocery store or drugstore, as if that were a thing you could even do in modern times.

On the other side of this coin (literally), you will give your grandchildren a nickel or a quarter and be all smug about it, as if that is a lot of money you've just given them. Tell them to go buy a comic book *and* a Ne-High Soda with it to thoroughly show just how out of touch you are, both economically *and* culturally.

How to Swear Like an Old Person

Even though life is pretty perfect for you as an Old Person — you're retired and have nothing but free time on your hands — you still might occasionally find yourself in moments of frustration. You might hear about something that's a real shame, or you perceive a young whipper-snapper disrespecting you, even though without you he'd be speaking German and Japanese! Or maybe the dang TV isn't pulling in a good reception, or your college's football team fumbles during the big game. For these unfortunate and fortunately rare moments, you need an expletive. But as a polite, civilized Old Person, you don't use profanity. You use one of these pre-approved Old Person Swears.

"For crying out loud!"

"You've got some nerve!"

"Well, I never!"

"Aw, heck!"

"Well, I'll be darned!"

"Fiddlesticks!"

"Goodness gracious!"

"What in the tarnation?"

"What in the Sam Hill?"

"Criminy!"

"For the love of Pete!"

"Jiminy Christmas!"

"Jiminy Cricket!"

"Oh dear!"

HOW TO HATE YOUNG PERSONS

Every story needs a hero, and in the story of America, that hero is you, Old Person. Through pure grit, determination, a system that favored middle-class, primarily white people, and a social safety net you thoroughly exploited until you killed it, you single-handedly built up a life for yourself and your fellow Old Persons. Now, you just want to enjoy it in peace and quiet, reminiscing about the way things used to be while puttering around the house and putting around the golf course, but these darn Young Persons just can't let that be. Every hero needs a villain, and for the Old Person, that villain is the Young Person.

Young Persons — *not* children and babies, which are wonderful (*see*, **Old Persons and Babies: Opposites Attract**), but adults in their twenties, thirties, and forties — just want to make life difficult for you, to make you accountable for all of the problems you caused, and to make you feel *bad*. Hey, the past is the past and shouldn't be brought up, unless we're talking about old baseball players or starlets with zowee gams. But these Young Persons just want to complain and complain about how they're poorly treated, or abused at work, or are the victims of systemic exploitation. Hey, you whiney youngin': Why not pick yourself up by your bootstraps and go to college? When we went to school, it was $8 a semester. That's the same price as one of your French avocado coffees or one of your Atari video games you shouldn't even be playing because *you're an adult.*

Then, once you're educated, you can get a nice job with a solid and noble corporation, like Pan Am or General Motors, stay there forever, and spend your money on the things you should be buying, meaning the things Old Persons know are the best things, like bar soap, fiber-rich cereal, and newspaper subscriptions.

"How About This Weather We've Been Having, Eh?"

For reasons that continue to baffle even the smartest oldologists down here at the Center of Oldological Technologies (C.O.O.T.), when a normal person turns into an Old Person, they take up an intense interest in a handful of particular intellectual pursuits, collectively referred to as the Elderly Sciences. Now, Old Persons aren't suddenly starting up chemistry labs in their spare bedrooms (no, that's still "the office" or "the computer room" or "the sewing room"). Rather, they might read an article, thumb through a paperback, or watch a documentary on TV about an enticing aspect of the world that is at least vaguely scientific in nature. This includes the fields of nutrition (what vitamins are best for building vitality in one's Old Person years), military history (World War II), and meteorology, or, in other words, *what's going on with this weather?*

This fascination likely stems from a place of settlement and settling. With the exception of RV-oriented Old Persons (*see,* **Get Yourself an RV!**), Old Persons have come to terms with the fact that they have settled into their house, their town, and their little communities, and they want to keep up with the hyper-local news. There's nothing more local than weather, particularly if it's going to rain today or not. Old Persons are *obsessed* with rainfall. It gives them something to celebrate, worry about, and discuss with other Old Persons. For example, if it rains, no matter the season or the number of rainy days in the past week, an Old Person is legally required to say, "It's raining! That's good, we needed it!" If it's cloudy, an Old Person has to announce, "Looks like rain." If it's sunny, an Old Person can either lament the lack of rainfall or celebrate the fact that it is finally not raining — it's up to them...or you!

How an Old Person acquires knowledge about the upcoming weather patterns is an old Old Person tool of the trade, but we're going to let you in on their secret, since you're now an Old Person. They watch the local news — an infallible source of meteorological knowledge, including a truly cutting-edge five-day forecast.

HOW TO TALK TO A YOUNG PERSON

Although you are an Old Person and loving it, you will still have to talk to younger individuals, particularly and probably almost exclusively your grandchildren. But they're so much younger than you, a completely different generation with its own standards of living and crazy slang terms you don't understand!

Fortunately, our researchers at C.O.O.T. have developed the *Whippersnapper Cycle*, a definitive guide for how to communicate with these strange creatures for effective and efficient information sharing.

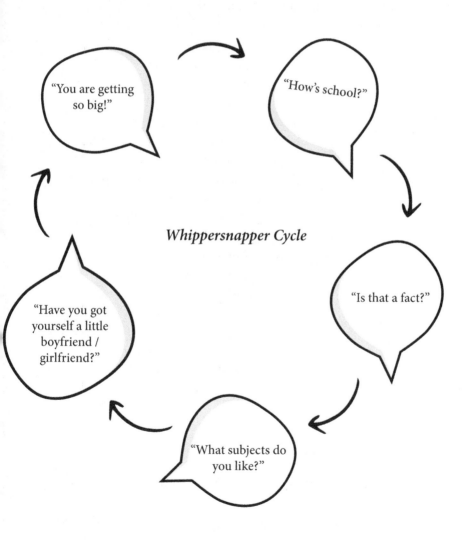

Whippersnapper Cycle

"You are getting so big!"

"How's school?"

"Is that a fact?"

"What subjects do you like?"

"Have you got yourself a little boyfriend / girlfriend?"

"THE"

It's formalizing, and Old Persons come from a generation that was aggressively more formal than the ones that came after it. Old Persons have a deep and abiding respect for institutions, and they show that by placing the definite article — the word "the" — in front of most any admirable person, institution, organization, or even concept. Why? Because they deserve that much.

Here are some things you'll come across in your daily life as an Old Person which you'll want to tell other Old Persons about. Can you determine which things should get a "the" in front of them?

_____ Google
_____ Fox News
_____ *Star Wars*
_____ TV
_____ Diabetes
_____ Cancer
_____ Safeway
_____ Barbies
_____ Music these days
_____ Facebook
_____ Church
_____ Young people these days
_____ Marital relations
_____ Video games
_____ Sports
_____ Mexicans
_____ Pizza

Answers:

Every single one of these items, and more, should get a "the" in front of them. You owe them that.

WISE WORDS OF THE OLD PERSON

Now that you're an Old Person, you've got a lifetime of wisdom to share, a vast collection of experiences from which to draw and make clever and profound observations about life, the world, and how things operate. Or, you could just trot out clichéd, hackneyed phrases that ring hollow but sound interesting. It's far easier than saying anything meaningful, important, or revelatory, all while making you seem smart and dignified!

*NOTE: If you preface each saying with "Well" and a pause, it will sound like you're really digging deep for these appropriate bon mots. The same effect can be achieved by adding a "you know" to the end of each saying.

"Give an inch, they'll take a mile."

"Teach a man to fish, he'll eat for a lifetime."

"The more things change, the more things stay the same."

"There's no accounting for taste."

"Don't count your chickens before they're hatched."

"Many hands make light work."

"Do what you love, and you'll never work a day in your life."

"A little hard work never killed anyone."

"A stitch in time saves nine."

"You catch more flies with honey than you do with vinegar."

"The early bird catches the worm."

"The squeaky wheel gets the grease."

"Don't judge a book by its cover."

"Too many cooks spoil the broth."

"A penny saved is a penny earned."

"Don't put the cart before the horse."

"Absence makes the heart grow fonder."

"You can lead a horse to water, but you can't make him drink."

"Beggars can't be choosers."

"We'll just have to cross that bridge when we come to it."

"Never look a gift horse in the mouth."

"When in Rome!"

"A bird in the hand is worth two in the bush."

"Breakfast is the most important meal of the day."

"Blood is thicker than water."

"Don't let yesterday take up too much of today."

"The road to Hell is paved with good intentions."

"Better safe than sorry."

"Even a broken clock is right twice a day!"

"Don't cry because it's over, smile because it happened."

"Tis better to have loved and lost than never to have loved at all."

"A fool and his money are soon parted."

"Variety is the spice of life."

Casual But Deeply-Held and Caustic Racism

If you've ever harbored progressive political beliefs, idealistic and inclusive attitudes, or just innate human decency, it's time to cast those foolish notions aside. You're an Old Person now, and that also means you're kind of a racist now.

Now that you're old and have experienced a lot of the world, you're oddly hostile toward much of it, such as races besides your own. Sure, it's counterintuitive to have lived a long life and gathered experiences and met thousands of people, then turn inward, paranoid, and afraid regarding people you know are not really that much different than you, but here we are.

When you're an Old Person, time is short and your brain is shriveled and things are harder to understand, so it saves time, energy, and mental effort to trade just in stereotypes. One ethnic group is "cheap," for example, while another is somehow both lazy *and* guilty of stealing jobs from hard-working Americans. You also resent people from any nation whose "behinds you saved in World War II" and don't trust any group involved with the development or production of computers, because clearly they're up to something.

Your newfound racist self, even though you fought the Nazis or marched in Civil Rights protests in the '60s, will also manifest itself in your word choice. You won't use full-on, common slurs to refer to how "[INSERT DEMOGRAPHIC HERE]" is ruining America, the world, or the youth of today, but rather semi-slurs, words that used to be okay to refer to large cultural swaths but are now so outdated that they seem offensive, as if you didn't learn the new terms on purpose. To you, it's perfectly fine to refer to anyone from Asia with the same word you'd use to describe a rug.

You will also now be expected to use old-fashioned, incredibly offensive names for certain objects or concepts. The words "conjoined twins" will never come out of your mouth, and you'll think it's fine to continue using the horrendous term people once called the football team in Washington, D.C. It's fine. You're old. *Things were different when you came up* will be your excuse and refrain.

Quiz: Are You **Really** the World's Greatest Grandpa?

Every male Old Person claims to be the World's Greatest Grandpa. That's quite a boast! But can you support your claim? Take this test to find out.

1. Do you have a name for your grandchild, such as "champ," "sport," "princess," or "big guy"?

If yes, continue. It not, stop. You are not the "World's Greatest Grandpa."

2. Have you said, "Here comes trouble!" or "They're gonna be a heartbreaker!" at the sight of your grandchildren?

If yes, continue. It not, stop. You are not the "World's Greatest Grandpa."

3. Have you, through some kind of magical power or trickery, produced a coin from your grandchild's ear, and then given it to said grandchild?

If yes, continue. It not, stop. You are not the "World's Greatest Grandpa."

4. Have you purchased a small amount of mild junk food for your grandchild, such as an ice cream cone, and then told them, "Don't tell your parents! This will be our little secret!"

If yes, continue. It not, stop. You are not the "World's Greatest Grandpa."

5. Has your grandchild made you a handmade card that you have kept on your refrigerator for in excess of nine months, or until it's completely broken down and falling apart?

If yes, continue. It not, stop. You are not the "World's Greatest Grandpa."

6. Do you own an article of clothing proclaiming your status as "World's Greatest Grandpa"?

If you have advanced *this* far, well, gosh, you really *are* the World's Greatest Grandpa. Congratulations!

Now, claim your prize: Print out this sign that says "World's Greatest Grandpa," laminate it, and tape it to your favorite mug to let people know!

THE OLD PERSON HALL OF FAME: GRANDMA!

Grandma is *the best*. Have you ever noticed that everybody in the whole wide world who grew up with a grandma thinks that their grandma is the best grandma in the whole wide world? We're going to let you in on a secret: *They're right.* Everybody's right. *You're* right. And *your grandkids* will be right. Because Grandma, the very concept and all who embody it, is unparalleled and is the greatest person who ever lived or ever shall live.

Going to grandma's house is a sacred ritual. It's where holidays are celebrated and where family traditions are learned, from Easter egg dying to Christmas morning rituals to what Thanksgiving foods to prepare each year to getting the scoop on which obscure relatives to despise and why. It's where Young Persons put their name on the bottom of artifacts you wish to inherit, and it's where kids go and hang out for a few days in the summer of glorious nothingness, of following their grandma around while she goes about her day. Grandma buys the sugar cereal that the parents won't. Grandma doesn't make you do chores. Grandma lets the kids watch soap operas. Grandma's hair is so unbelievably and impossibly silver.

Grandma, in short, rules.

Chapter Two
Of Sound Old Body and Sound Old Mind

Your Old Person body and mind may not work as well as they once did, so here's a primer on getting used to it. WE SAID YOUR BODY AND MIND MAY NOT WORK AS WELL AS THEY ONCE DID. BECAUSE YOU'RE AN OLD PERSON NOW!

THAT OLD PERSON SMELL

Perhaps the most quintessential — and famous — Old Person characteristic is that Old Person Smell. Us scientists at the the Center of Oldological Technologies (C.O.O.T.) have conducted several extensive studies on why Old Persons smell the way they do, that foul collection of scents that you won't actually be able to smell when you're an Old Person because 1) your ability to smell isn't so great when you're old, and 2) you can't smell your own house smell or body odor. It's a biological fact.

So what is that Old Person Smell, exactly? It's a combination of body odor and bad breath caused by slowly dying and failing bodily systems, along with the generous application of Old Person health and beauty products, the cooking of Old Person food, terrible artificial air fresheners, and, most notably, small pets that don't get bathed enough because it's hard for an Old Person to bathe a little dog or a cranky kitty.

And so, to complete the full Old Person Smell *scent profile*, you must get an Old Person appropriate pet. What's that, you say you already have a pet? That just won't do. You'll have to give them away to your adult children or the pound, because the only kind of pets Old Persons are permitted to have are a tiny, awful dog — one of those white ones that are hard to pet and have a bunch of crusty junk on their eyes all the time — or three cats. No more, no less. *Three cats.* One dog or three cats provides just the right amount of odor to complete the Old Person Smell.

The final piece of the Old Person Smell: a touch of Werther's Original, which, as an Old Person, you have on hand at all times, for a sweet little reward or when you need to "wet your whistle" (*see,* **Candy is Dandy**). It provides just enough kick for an early afternoon pick-me-up and is responsible for that hint of sweetness in Old Person Smell.

Toot-Toot-Tootsie!

Old Persons and flatulence go together like Old Persons and prunes — it's a natural, healthy fit that involves, well, *something* making a hasty and unpleasant retreat from "down below." Yes, we're getting a bit uncharacteristically ribald here, but you read that correctly. To be frank, Old Persons fart, and they fart *a lot*. It's just the way it is.

Over decades of regular digestion, bowel movements, and low-to-moderate everyday flatulence, an Old Person's rear-end exit hole is no longer small and tight, but rather quite loose, allowing plenty of gas to escape all through the day and all through the night. It doesn't seem to matter what Old Persons eat; even if they enjoy a diet rich in non-fart-causing foods, they still tend to fart with great regularity and abundance. However, the standard Old Person diet, heavy on the fiber, flavorless roughage, and hard boiled eggs, certainly doesn't make things any better.

In short, you, as an Old Person, can no longer control every action of your bowels, and that makes you a little gassy. Those farts are a contributing factor to that distinctive Old Person Smell™ (*see*, **That Old Person Smell**), but surprisingly, not all that much. Old Person farting as it actually affects the Old Person's life is mainly as a means to an end, an excuse for humor and allusion, or to justify the purchase of cloying potpourris and canned air fresheners. For example, you may ask your doctor about your "gas" or "toots" or "wind," or chuckle at those "Old Fart" slippers in the mail order novelty catalog that make little fart sounds when you walk.

As far as the former is concerned, Old Persons pride themselves on their cleverness and manners, so they would never openly discuss farting. It's your right as an Old Person to just let them rip, and you can get away with it, pretending that you yourself didn't smell *or* hear the release of the most toxic gas since you fought in the European Theater in 1943. Nobody is going to call you out — they don't want to embarrass or disrespect you, the Old Person.

That means toot away, friend!

Oopsies!

As vivacious as you feel, or how relatively young you look, whether you're out there power-walking through the mall or letting that closely cropped silver hair dance in the wind when you take a Sunday drive in your convertible, you are old. You are an Old Person. That carries with it some burdens, most of them physical, but a few of which are mental. For example, there's the issue of forgetfulness. It just happens. But hey, don't worry about it. People forget things. "Pobody's Nerfect," as that fun hat says, the one you bought in a gift shop on a vacation. (What vacation? You can't remember.)

Really, it's fine. Forgetfulness is in no way a serious and unquestionable signifier that aging is happening, that the fringes of the endgame of your life are coming into view. Not remembering or forgetting what you're talking about is just a cute little thing that Old Persons do. It's definitely not the first sign of dementia, a disease that will rob you of your faculties, and, more cruelly, the memories of your magnificent life and loved ones.

You have power over this and don't have to dwell on the frightening and inevitable march of time and progressive illness. You can call these signs of dementia and slow brain death "Oopsies." Or "blips." Or, if you're feeling a little naughty, "brain farts." It's all up to you.

We also recommend "senior moments." It just sounds fun! It harkens back to snapshots taken in your varsity high school yearbook letterman sweater days, juxtaposing a concept of youth with the cruel heartbreak of aging.

EVER HAVE A 'SENIOR MOMENT'? IF, AS AN OLD PERSON, YOU HAVEN'T YET, YOU SOON WILL. A 'SENIOR MOMENT' IS WHEN YOU COMPLETELY FORGET A PREVIOUSLY WELL-KNOWN BIT OF INFORMATION, CAN'T RECALL A MEMORY, CAN'T REMEMBER THE REASON YOU WALKED INTO THE ROOM, OR JUST TRAIL OFF MIDWAY THROUGH A SENTENCE, HAVING LOST THE THREAD. WE CALL THESE 'SENIOR MOMENTS' BECAUSE THEY'RE SOMETHING EVERY OLD PERSON GOES THROUGH. WELCOME TO THE CLUB!

Now, why don't you go back up to the top and read this article again.

Adult Diapers and Colostomy Bags

You know when leaving the house, up to this point, you would ritualistically check your pockets or purse to make sure you had your wallet, keys, and phone on you? As an Old Person, you will still have to do that, only with some adjustments, and some additional, just for Old Persons accessories you almost literally can't leave home without.

As an Old Person, you've probably noticed that your body has at least slowly or mildly started to fail you in various ways, such as your newfound inability to keep all of your urine inside of your body for anything more than 10 minutes. The solution: adult diapers. They slip on just like regular underwear, and they're thin and unnoticeable just like regular underwear, but unlike regular underwear, you're allowed — if not encouraged — to let that tinkle drip, flow, gush, and rest. It's no problem!

For those who are a little bit more of an older Old Person and, well, having a little trouble around the corner where fudge is made, there's the colostomy bag. And to think, this whole time you've been holding your stool inside of your colon and letting it out when you gain access to a toilet like some kind of chump!

And when you get back home and prepare to go to bed for the night, don't forget to put on your CPAP machine. It's like snorkeling...in bed!

Stay Sharp!

Let's get real here about one hard truth of aging: As an Old Person, your ol' noggin isn't quite what it used to be (*see,* **Oopsies!**). You might trail off in the middle of a sentence, or forget why you went into a room, or can't recall the name of the old friend you ran into at church. This is a sad but natural progression, but one that you can hold off, at least for a while. Now that you're actually an Old Person, it's time to start thinking about ways to prevent the degradation of your mental agility for when you're an even older Old Person.

Is it too late already? Probably! Will these solutions convince you you're doing something positive for yourself anyway? Sure! And hey, it's all about killing time until you can no longer hold your mouth closed.

Wheel of Fortune
You were going to watch every night anyway, you Old Person you. But playing along at home, guessing letters and the answer to the puzzle and such, is a great way to stay sharp.

Crosswords
Proof that newspapers only cater to Old Persons — they're loaded with these brain-challenging word puzzles. Look around, and you'll also find a word jumble or two.

Chinese Checkers
It takes a keen eye and a keen mind to beat your grandchild at this classic board game!

Murder Mysteries
Can you guess the murderer before the TV detective does? Yes you can!

Vitamins
Make sure to regularly take those non-FDA approved brain-boosting supplements they advertise on talk radio and afternoon television.

> ALL THE THINGS YOU CAN CALL SUDOKU, A STRANGE AND FOREIGN-SOUNDING WORD:
>
> SUZY Q
> SOO-DEE-DOO-DEE
> SUKIYAKI
> JAPANESE NUMBER GAME
> SUDUKU
> SODOKOO
> SACKY YUCKY
> SACKY HACKY

MOBILITY DEVICES CAN HELP YOU HELP YOURSELF

Let's face the facts, here: you're an Old Person now, and you're not as agile as you once were. Yep, there's no doubt about it, almost instantly upon becoming an Old Person, well, the old gray mare, she ain't what she used to be, so to speak. And those old bones and joints of yours quickly and rapidly descend into the territory that both doctors and calcium supplement manufacturers call "rickety."

There's just no way to fully prevent or stave off the ricketyfying of an Old Person's old bones, and their subsequent diminished capacity to bend and move. (Apart from those calcium supplements that you, as an Old Person, will take daily thinking they do good, washed down with a glass of delicious whole milk.) But not all hope is lost. You don't have to be a shut-in, hunched over as you shuffle about the house in your slippers calling out, "Oh, darn these old bones!" to everyone or no one in particular. You're an Old Person fortunate enough to live in the future, and the future is a time of mobility scooters. How would you like to have your freedom back, or as the case may be, to still have a shred of it? Then a mobility scooter is for you. It looks, feels, and acts just like a motorcycle, if a motorcycle had an additional back wheel for extra support, ran on an inefficient rechargeable battery, did a top speed of 5 miles per hour, and had a little basket on the front of it, just like the bicycle you got for your ninth birthday during The Good Old Days.

Add one of those stretchy arm-claw things, and you'll be able to get any item from any shelf down at the pharmacy. And while you're at the pharmacy, grab a brochure to see about home installation of one of those elevator chairs you can put on your stairwell, making you just as mobile at home as you are at the store.

FOR VERY MATURE AUDIENCES ONLY: EROTICA FOR OLD PERSONS

It was a day like any other, the day she came into my life. I was sitting on my chair that rocks — not too little, not too much — out on my front porch. I was listening to Paul Harvey and waiting for the daily arrival of the mail, and also making sure that none of these damn neighborhood kids set foot on my beautiful lawn. I had my cane and fist ready to shake if I needed to, so let's just say I wasn't in the mood for love.

But then she walked by.

Ca-thunk, ca-thunk, swish-swish.

Her walker struck the ground first, then again, and then her Keds-covered feet shuffled along behind it to keep up. The sound caught my attention, but her looks held it.

She looked like she'd been a real looker back in the day. A real tomato, if you know what I mean. She wore a floral-print dress that went all the way down, thoroughly covering up what I assumed was once a real nice figure. A busty, big-hipped gal. At one point, those gams must have gone all the way up. Ha-cha-cha.

She reminded me of a pinup I had in my foot locker when I fought with distinction in one of the wars. As she slowly made her way down the street, ignoring my whistles and cat-calls — uninterested and aloof, or perhaps unable to hear them — I thought about what it must have been like to neck with her in the back of a car up on Overlook Point. How we would have pawed at each other. Undershirts and girdles and slips and skivvies all tangled in a pile while she made me feel like a real man, a genuine hunk like Tab

> EVER HAVE A 'SENIOR MOMENT'? IF, AS AN OLD PERSON, YOU HAVEN'T YET, YOU SOON WILL. A 'SENIOR MOMENT' IS WHEN YOU COMPLETELY FORGET A PREVIOUSLY WELL-KNOWN BIT OF INFORMATION, CAN'T RECALL A MEMORY, CAN'T REMEMBER THE REASON YOU WALKED INTO THE ROOM, OR JUST TRAIL OFF MIDWAY THROUGH A SENTENCE, HAVING LOST THE THREAD. WE CALL THESE 'SENIOR MOMENTS' BECAUSE THEY'RE SOMETHING EVERY OLD PERSON GOES THROUGH. WELCOME TO THE CLUB!

Hunter or Rock Hudson.

But she still excited me. If she wanted me to, and by which I mean, if she'd heard my whistles and cat-calls, I'd take out my dentures, ostomy bag, and hearing aid and give her the ol' what-for.

I bet she smells like White Shoulders and Vap-O-Rub.

Oh, what I would do to her in the stateroom of an affordably priced cruise ship after a hearty supper of liver.

That's a Scam! (Or Is It?)

Before you take both of your bony, wrinkled, veiny feet and dive right into the world of Old Persons, we need to get a baseline reading of where you're at, brain-wise. In order to properly enjoy the Old Person lifestyle, you have to be in the proper Old Person frame of mind. Old Persons are frequently the targets of scams, as they are perceived as gullible old coots who can be easily emotionally and intellectually manipulated. But they're not going to pull one over on *you*! And we're going to help. In the following scenarios, identify which are genuine, legitimate, and on-the-level business transactions and which are complete and total scams designed to separate you from your pension, savings, and Social Security checks.

1. When someone claiming to be "your grandson" calls and says they're in "a lot of trouble" and they need you to wire them some money as soon as possible.

☐ **That's all well and good**
☐ **That's a scam!**

2. Nutritional supplements sold not in stores, but via a toll-free number advertised on right-wing talk radio.

☐ **That's all well and good**
☐ **That's a scam!**

3. A voicemail on the answering machine about how your car's warranty has expired.

☐ **That's all well and good**
☐ **That's a scam!**

4. An inquiry that will tell you if you have unclaimed money owed to you, and all they need to check is your Social Security Number, your bank account number, and routing number.

☐ **That's all well and good**
☐ **That's a scam!**

5. Medicare pharmacy discount card sold in a TV commercial with a name like Liberty Union or Union Liberty, and it's only $99.

☐   **That's all well and good**
☐   **That's a scam!**

6. Pop-up ad on the computer that says you've got viruses and it will only cost $200 to fix it right now

☐   **That's all well and good**
☐   **That's a scam!**

7. News of a vaguely defined sweepstakes, but you *won*!

☐   **That's all well and good**
☐   **That's a scam!**

8. When the Amazon website on the computer needs your credit card information.

☐   **That's all well and good**
☐   **That's a scam!**

9. How the phone company is supposedly increasing its monthly charge by $1 after five years.

☐   **That's all well and good**
☐   **That's a scam!**

10. Your adult child taking power of attorney over your financial affairs.

☐   **That's all well and good**
☐   **That's a scam!**

11. The cell phone store that says it can fix your cell phone.

☐   **That's all well and good**
☐   **That's a scam!**

12. Warranties.

☐ **That's all well and good**
☐ **That's a scam!**

Answers:

Nos. 1 through 7: All are legitimate. Give whoever asks all of the money they want and whatever personal information they ask for, so that they can help you!

Nos. 8 through 12: Scams, scams, scams! That's how they get ya!

Old Persons and Babies: Opposites Attract

Scientific research and surveys conducted by several oldology think tanks have found that an Old Person's hatred of different age groups varies greatly, depending on the age. For example, Old Persons harbor negligible hate toward other Old Persons (except for those who have better lawns and bigger RVs) and intense animosity toward teens and twenty-somethings. The only age group besides Old Persons that Old Persons genuinely like and appreciate: children aged 0 to 3, or, colloquially, babies.

This psychology is counterintuitive on first glance, but that's only if one ignores strong circumstantial evidence of the bond, however unlikely, that Old Persons have with babies.

1. Babies are the successful physical manifestation of years of browbeating their own adult children into "giving them some grandkids." The Old Person feels full of worth, knowing that their otherwise autonomous adult children did what they told them to do.

2. Babies represent legacy and a carrying on of the family name and genetics. A baby related to the Old Person is the Old Person made new and will live on long after the Old Person is dead. This makes an Old Person smile a little Old Person smile.

3. It's an old joke, but it's rooted in truth: Old Persons like babies because babies are just tiny Old Persons — they're hairless, helpless, powerless, eat soft food, and can't control their bodily functions. The only thing missing is wrinkles.

Furthermore, babies are new and fresh, as opposed to Old Persons, who are anything but those two things. Old Persons crave the life force of the babies and subconsciously try to consume it whenever they're around. Old Persons wish to eat the souls of babies so that they may live a while longer. (It's not like they even know they're doing it, but they are.)

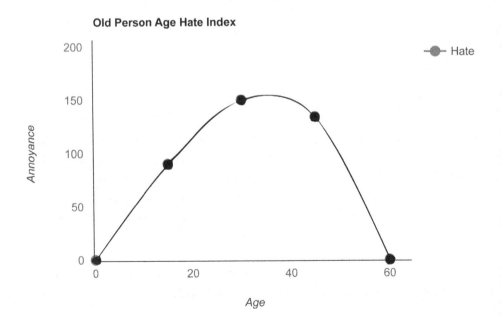

DEMANDING TO KNOW THE DETAILS OF THE NEXT VISIT

Happy people, free spirits, and those darn Young Persons all will tell you that the key to contentment and enjoying life is to "live in the moment." That's all very well and good…if you're a spritely kid of 55. But you're an Old Person, and you don't have time to waste living in the moment. You've got to know what's going to happen and when, and *you need to know right now!*

That's why, when you're enjoying a personal visit or phone call from a relative, such as a grown child or their precious children — *your grandbabies* — it's important to spend at least half of the visit or phone call discussing when will be the next time that you see them or talk with them. It matters not that you're in the midst of seeing them or talking with them — all that matters is tomorrow. Because there might not be a tomorrow with which you can fret about another tomorrow.

THE OLD PERSON HALL OF FAME: JOE BIDEN

Plenty of *old men* have been president — everyone but JFK and Obama —but it's been a long time since an *Old Person* was president. That's why it was so refreshing when Joe Biden finally capped off a lifetime of being the definitive Old Person politician and landed the highest elected office in the land. Politics aside, Joe Biden is a true Old Person. He's just one of us. For example:

• He's got an often-stated, unabashed love of trains.

• He seems like the kind of guy who calls everybody "Champ."

• He loves diners.

• He's been rocking that silver fox hairdo for at least 40 years.

• He loves going to church.

• He refers to his wife as "the boss" and totally means it.

• He loves a good handshake, back slap, or casual touch. Old Persons' love language is definitely the kind of touching one does at business meetings or weddings in 1960.

• He fancies himself a straight shooter who tells it like it is, enjoying that privilege that can only come from being a white Old Person.

Chapter Three
Get Up and Get Out There!

You might be dead soon, but you're not dead yet, you know. Throw off that caftan, grab your cane, and get ready to thrive and be truly alive!

MALL WALKING

Not only does walking around the perimeter of a mall burn as many as 30 calories in a single hour, it allows you, as an Old Person, the rare privilege of being out in public. It's a great arrangement! Not only is it free (important when you're on a fixed income), but you get to exercise in a *gorgeous* shopping pavilion.

And since the mall-walking hours are scheduled before the mall is open for general business, you'll avoid the natural predators of the Old Person, which also happen to be the mall's worst denizens: teenagers, gang members, high-pressure salesmen, and laze-abouts. The early hour is also a boon should you get lost—it's much easier for the authorities to find you in an empty mall than it is in a full one filled with teenagers, gang members, high-pressure salesmen, and laze-abouts.

If you live in one of the 98 percent of American cities where there no longer is a safe shopping mall or one that's open, well, first of all, that's a shame! But there are other things you can do to keep fit and stay active. Consider a water aerobics class at your YMCA affiliate or just going for a walk through the neighborhood, but with a couple of walking poles that absolutely do not make you look ridiculous.

Church!

As an Old Person, you are also now a religious person. It doesn't matter in what faith you were raised, or what denomination you followed as a Middle Aged Person — you're an Old Person now, and you attend a Catholic, Lutheran, Methodist, or Presbyterian church. *Those are your options.*

More so than your spiritual development — that doesn't really matter anymore, as you're either heaven-or-hell-bound at this point and you don't have a lot of time to change either trajectory — church offers so many things that Old Persons love more than teenagers love disrespecting their elders and wearing baggy pants combined. To name just a few of those delights, when you attend a church service on Sunday morning, you get to wear a pretty dress with flowers on it or a suit from your old businessman days and drive the car to a lovely building, and when you get there, you get to sit down for an hour. Throw a few coins in the collection plate to feel generous and charitable, and then you get to listen to the blandest and therefore most beautiful music there is, all in praise of the Lord. That's another thing — Old Persons *love* authority figures and respectable members of the community. Church instills both a fear of God, the ultimate authority figure, as well as a reverence for reverends. (And they always tell such funny jokes in their sermons!)

But after church? That's where the party happens. Head over to the community room for the ideal Old Person snack: a Styrofoam cup of weak coffee (*see,* **Care for a Cup of Joe?**) and half of a stale, plain cake doughnut. All your Old Person friends will be there, and you can talk to them about which of your friends aren't there, due to death and sickness, and how that is such a shame. And then after the after-party, you might just take the long way home in the car and have a nice Sunday drive.

And besides, church is how you get good with God! You'll want to make sure you're headed for Heaven, which is pretty much just an old folks home…but one of the nice ones.

Community Theater

Who doesn't love an evening at *the theater*, or, if we're feeling fancy (because we are when we're going out at night to see a stageplay or a musical comedy), the *theatre*? Certainly Old Persons do. Old Persons, such as yourself, love theater, so long as it is quaint, familiar, mildly amusing, and not at all provocative. In other words, *nice*. Old Persons like plays and musicals (but calling them by outdated terms like stageplays and musical comedies) that were first staged in the mid-20th century and are nice.

Where can one find entertainments that fit this criteria? Why, at the 1964 Tony Awards broadcast, or, more readily, at a local community theater, of course, where non-professional actors well over the age of 50 perform the same plays as the local high school's drama club and with the same level of talent.

Old Persons just love community theater. After all, it's a nice night out, and sometimes it's a real hoot to leave the house at 6 p.m. instead of being home for the night and in your PJs by that hour. Also, it's culture, but not "stuffy" culture like the opera or the ballet. It's also nostalgic, because community theaters only present nice stageplays and musical comedies about olden times, ones about nice sons coming to dinner, or love letters, or two adorable people falling in love, or a Scottish town that only exists once a century. Plus, you can brag to your friends about being a subscriber of a particular community theater, or float the possibility of taking out-of-town guests to a show there.

> **Remember...**
>
> DURING LULLS OR BORING MOMENTS IN THE PRODUCTION, YOU CAN FANTASIZE ABOUT BEING SUCH A TOP NOTCH PATRON THAT YOU CAN GET YOUR NAME ON A SEAT WHEN YOU DIE!

By the way, next month, *your* local community theater is doing *Damn Yankees*, just like the one you saw in the big city that one time. Kim Novak was in the movie, and she's just darling!

A TRIP TO THE DOCTOR'S OFFICE, OR THE BIG DAY

A poem by Earl Henry "Bud" Johnson, retired

Awaken my love, let's sleep in no more,

For I've got the perfect Old Person day in store.

You must see your doctor, and I must see mine,

They'll tell us to change things, but we'll insist that we're fine.

Ours don't come until 10:45,

So we should leave rather early to ensure we arrive

In plenty of time, in case traffic is wild,

Although our condo is no more than a mile

Away from the medical office, that's why we moved here.

When was that again? Six months ago? A year?

We'll leave right away, just as soon as you're dressed.

Come on, up and at 'em! You're getting me stressed!

Your makeup looks fine, I've seen you much worse.

Let's get a move on, Frances, grab your cane and your purse!

There's no time for breakfast, a nectarine will suffice.

Now, off with the nightgown (I won't tell you twice)!

I'll be in the car, I'll be honking the horn

While you take your time, just wasting the morn.

That's great! You're all ready, I'm ready to drive!

We'll be in the parking lot by 7:45.

Inside the Old Person's Car

Here's what your car will look like now, Old Person. So get out there and have fun, and do your best not to plow through a crowded farmer's market!

- Too short to properly see over wheel now
- Blistering hot coffee in paper cup with no lid in cupholder
- Various air fresheners, religious items, and novelties hanging from review mirror
- Unfolded map on dashboard (Old Persons *never* use GPS)
- Sun visor all the way down with numerous receipts and long-disused garage door opener

Get Yourself an RV!

Old Persons like big cars. The larger a car is, the more status it conveys, the more expensive it is (at least that's how it used to be), and the more power it's got under the hood. Plus, it takes up more room, to which you are entitled. And nothing gets the neighbors more jealous than a big, honking Cadillac, Plymouth, or Oldsmobile.

But when those big boats aren't big enough, you've got to go *bigger*.

You've gotten to the age where you still want to go on adventures, even camping, but you just don't have it in you anymore to be roughing it. You like to be comfortable, and there's nothing wrong with that. So even when you're camping or having adventures, why not take the creature comforts of home along with you: Buy a recreational vehicle (or "RV"), your home away from home with everything from home still in it. It might cost your life savings, but it will feel reassuring to screw your kids out of their inheritance by spending $100,000 on something that's going to be dated and dingy in a few weeks and will be an eyesore in your driveway that will piss off your neighbors, who aren't doing a very good job of masking their jealousy.

And you really should have no business being on the road in that thing — it's the size of an apartment building — and yet you, an Old Person with poor eyesight and slow reflexes, is driving the thing. It's a recipe for fun, and it's something to which you have every right to do!

The Old Person on Vacation

Scowl (to note disdain for Young Persons and foreign things)

Sunglasses (the kind that fit *over* the glasses)

Sunblock (on nose, not rubbed in)

Floppy hat (to keep sun out of eyes and protect bald spot)

Ill-fitting golf shirt

Ill-fitting khaki shorts

Money belt (full of travelers checks)

Fanny pack (for diabetes medicine, hotel room key)

Camera bag (for very large film camera)

Crocs (for comfort)

Is That the Bookmobile or the Senior Bus?

Picture this, Old Person: You're standing outside your modest, ranch-style home or senior living facility, near the curb — but not too close to the edge, and certainly not on your precious lawn (*see,* **On Getting Others Off Your Lawn: An Old Person Call to Action**) —waiting in anxious anticipation for when you can finally spot it, down the street in the distance, just past where you can make it out. Your eyes aren't as good as they used to be, of course, so you can't quite tell *what* exactly that slowly moving amorphous blob even is. But you can instantly narrow it to down to two options, and you're likely waiting on one or the other. That white thing, edging closer to you at 20 miles per hour, is either your local library's "bookmobile" or the transport bus for seniors only.

Here's an easy reference guide to have on hand so you can figure out whether or not to get your hopes up as you await the arrival of whatever white vehicle it is.

What are all those gadgets?
Both the bookmobile and the senior shuttle have a lot of doodads and fancy gadgets on-board. Look closely when the doors open. Are all those jigamabobs just metal bars to keep books from falling off of shelves, and maybe also they've got the computer in there? Then that's a bookmobile, because the books need to stay in place and they use that darn computer to check out your books these days instead of stamping the little card in the back like they used to do. If the thingy is just a big wheelchair lifter, then you're looking at the senior shuttle.

How many people are in there?
If there's just one person, that's the driver of the bookmobile. If there are a bunch of fellow Old Persons in there, it's the senior shuttle.

How many books are in there?
If it's positively filled with books, it's a bookmobile. If the only books you see are mystery novels in the laps of your Old Person friends, it's the elderly van.

What does the signage say?
If the words written on the side read something like "Books 2 Go" or "Books on the Move," in a clearly-printed boxy font, it's the bookmobile. If the words written on the side of the vehicle appear in a script typeface and include the words "Senior," "Golden," or "Silver," it's the senior shuttle.

"Can I Write You a Check?"

Writing a check just might be the best Old Person activity because it encompasses so many other qualities, skills, and actions that an Old Person loves.

• It includes a careful balancing of funds — money going in and money going out — and all Old Persons love to obsess over money, because they are retired and on a fixed income, even though they are more than financially stable enough to have retired in the first place.

• Writing a check wastes others' time *and* the Old Person's. Filling one out takes time, as does giving it to a clerk that has to process it, and because they do it so rarely, it eats up even more time. That kills a few more minutes of the long, empty day of an Old Person but uses a few moments in the lives of the other people waiting in line at the store behind the Old Person. They *could* use that time to chit-chat with you, Old Person!

• Those special little pull-out shelves by the register are unnecessary and a little treat. Little desks are something Old Persons love (they call them *credenzas*), as is feeling special.

• Checks require the use of Cursive, which is the official written language of Old Persons everywhere.

SOME THOUGHTS ON TECHNOLOGY

The older of an Old Person you become, the more you hate anything new; the newer it is, the more you hate it. And there's nothing newer, and continuously, unrelentingly newer and renewing, than technology. Sure, it's all supposed to save labor and make our lives easier, but what about the labor and difficulty of learning how to use all those new electric doodads and automatic gizmos?

You see, as an Old Person, it's difficult to learn things. According to oldologists, this is on account of how, after seven or more decades of absorbing life, memories, and information, an Old Person's brain is almost entirely filled up and becomes incapable of storing new instructions on how to use, for example, a "smart" phone, "digital" camera, or that thing at the grocery store where you put in your bank card.

Also affecting the Old Person's ability to learn technology: willful ignorance. As an Old Person, you've earned the right to reject anything new, dismiss it outright, and bemoan it as a sign of the rapidly changing times into a dystopian, nightmarish world that lacks human interaction and glorious time-wasting. It's just so much easier to reject it all and cling tenaciously to the things you know than it is to evolve, endure a learning curve, and admit one's failings. Complete and utter arrogance to your own detriment — now you're thinking like an Old Person.

This gives you the right, duty, and responsibility to appear incredibly confused by every new gadget that comes your way. Sure, pretend you don't know how to take a picture on an iPhone — that's you taking up space and standing up for the old ways, even though it works just like every other camera ever. Make a big fuss and ask for help when using the ATM payment system at the grocery store, even though there's no way you haven't yet encountered and mastered this piece of technology embedded in society for more than 30 years. You certainly don't need — or will barely use, deeply distrust, or bother to learn — how to use streaming television, a computer, or a CPAP machine.

All tech is bad. Well, except the iPad. That's your everything now. It can take pictures and you can read large-print eBooks on it!

Chapter Four
What's Cookin', Good Lookin'?

What does being an Old Person taste like? Well, it's pretty delicious! Let's learn all about the soft and bland delights that await your mouth and tummy.

Start Your Day the Old Person Way!

Grapefruit. The Official Breakfast Food of Old Persons. It's fruit, so it's healthy, but also not too sweet and makes your lips all puckered and withered, like an Old Person's ought to be. You're probably not supposed to eat this because it counteracts all 11 of your prescription drugs, but we won't tell your doctor if you won't!

A single hard-boiled egg. An excellent source of protein — bland, flavorless, rubbery, nauseating protein.

Oatmeal. Gumming down this mush will give you all the energy you need for a day of doing nothing and being cranky!

Empty side plate. This is where the bacon and sausage you want to eat used to sit. *Sigh.*

Whole wheat toast. The more burnt it is, the longer it takes you to eat, thus killing precious time.

Prune juice. Stay regular, friends!

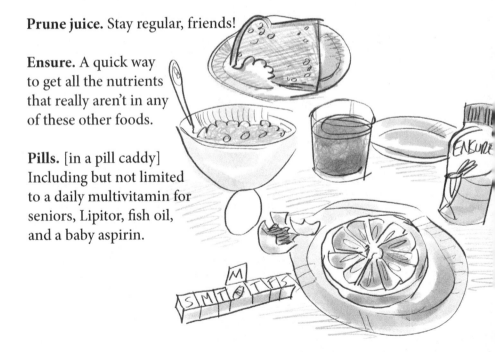

Ensure. A quick way to get all the nutrients that really aren't in any of these other foods.

Pills. [in a pill caddy] Including but not limited to a daily multivitamin for seniors, Lipitor, fish oil, and a baby aspirin.

Care for a Cup of Joe?

Coffee is big in American society, and it has been for a long time, although what it looks like has changed. From shoveling spoonfuls of what looked and tasted like bitter dirt into stovetop percolators, to Mr. Coffee automatic machines, to the espresso and frou-frou Starbucks-type beverages of today, coffee has evolved. But not if you're an Old Person. The idea of what coffee is thoroughly stuck in the past for you, where it belongs, but it also extends its influence to many other areas of your life.

Being an Old Person means wiling away what little time you have left on this earth by filling your days with mindless rituals and routines. Your morning coffee ordeal can take care of some of that. Even though you're only going to drink one cup, because too much makes you nervous, or have to use the restroom, or unable to sleep 14 hours after consumption, you should still make it count.

REMEMBER...
THIS ALL CAN BE AVOIDED IF YOU'RE AN OLD PERSON WHO GETS COFFEE WITH OTHER OLD PERSONS AT THE MCDONALD'S AT 6 A.M. EVERY MORNING AND JUST HANGS OUT THERE WITH THE FELLAS OR GALS, DISCUSSING THE GOOD OLD DAYS, CONSERVATIVE POLITICS, AND HOW THESE KIDS TODAY WITH THE SKATEBOARDS AND ROCK MUSIC HAVE NO DARN MANNERS.

1. When using your yellowed Mr. Coffee machine with the blinking "12:00" clock you purchased 35 years ago, make sure to brew it extra weak — one small scoop into the filter basket and then fill up the chamber with as much tap water as it will take.

2. Get your accessories ready: a dainty sugar bowl filled with crusty sugar and a spoon you can just leave in there.

3. With sugar comes cream or, if you're an Old Person, that weird Coffee-Mate powder they have in tire stores and at AA meetings, or the milk-like refrigerated stuff made from vegetable oil, corn syrup, and assorted artificial flavors. So creamy!

4. Take an hour to drink your coffee, until it is cold. Throw the rest of the pot away by pouring it down the drain.

5. Save your coffee craving for a piece or two of coffee-flavored hard candy, which you will keep in a little dish in the living room or in your purse or pants pocket.

6. Save the coffee can — your coffee definitely comes in a can — for nails, pennies, and other random household artifacts.

Your Old Person Spice Rack

Before you were an Old Person Spice Rack

Old Person Spice Rack

A Taste of Grandma That Will Linger Forever

Now that you're an Old Person, you're responsible for writing down all your beloved recipes so that your descendants can make them in the future (but *never* as good as you could). It's like you'll live forever with your severe, cursive handwriting on a brittle, yellowed, and stained index card kept in a tiny wooden box. We've gotten you started with one ultimate, mega-old-fashioned recipe that is every classic homemade dessert all rolled into one, with all manner of wonderful ingredients you'll definitely be able to find in this day and age.

Recipe

Grandma's Mock Shoofly Chess Pie Cake Surprise

1/4 tsp cream of Kyhfssjue
Handful of curds
1/4 cup oleomargarine
2 cups bulger
1 can peaches in heavy syrup
1 jar molasses
1 bottle light corn syrup
1 bottle dark corn syrup
Dusting of cornmeal
2/3 cup powdered milk
3 shirred eggs
1–2 cups schmaltz
1 cup finely diced celery
Cup of chicory coffee, cooled
Raisins
Cytamens
Assorted unsalted nuts
Shortening
Bouillon cubes

1 tablespoon velvet
1 can cheery pie filling
4 ounces saved bacon grease
Three small jars mincemeat
1 can cherry pie filling
6 ounces buttermilk
3 bufudgdcs

1. Preheat oven to 350 degrees.

2. Sift all dry together, mix all wet. Gently fold the dry into the wet.

3. Pour into Bundt pan.

4. Bake until done.

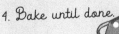

4:30 P.M.: SUPPER TIME!

Old Persons like bargains, and the reasons are twofold. First, it's satisfying to think that you've learned something over your many years doddering around this great big world, like knowing how to sniff out a good deal, or maybe just not wasting money when you don't have to. Secondly, as an Old Person and, additionally, a retiree, you're on a fixed income. More than just a phrase Old Persons say all the time at the slightest provocation to describe and explain their financial status, a fixed income means bargains are necessary for the Old Person wishing to live as high on the hog as possible.

This is all precisely why today's savvy Old Person loves to eat their night-time meal, supper, at about half past four p.m. (They're also just plain hungry — Old Persons start their day no later than 6 a.m., so as not to "sleep the day away," and by the time the late afternoon rolls around, they're positively famished.)

> **REMEMBER...**
> TO THE OLD PERSON GENERATION, 'SUPPER' MEANS DINNER AND 'DINNER' MEANS LUNCH. ADDITIONALLY, THERE IS NO SUCH THING AS BRUNCH FOR OLD PERSONS, AND TEA TIME IS A LATE-DINNER, EARLY-SUPPER CONSISTING OF LITTLE SANDWICHES AND SWEET TREATS, CONSUMED EXACTLY ONCE ON A VACATION TO LONDON, OR VICTORIA, BRITISH COLUMBIA.

Once upon a time, America's now dying diner landscape offered the Early Bird Special, intended to bring in customers during the slow period between lunch and dinner rushes, approximately four to five p.m. These specials were a specific, set menu item or set meal, but deeply discounted. Today's restaurants don't necessarily offer cheaper meals prior to the dinner period, but Old Persons continue to go to restaurants at 4:30 in the afternoon. Oldologists cite this as a fascinating example of Old Person instinct, an instinct you now have. And that instinct tells you that 4:30 is time for soup and mush, which you will only eat a little of and complain that it is too rich and/or salty anyway.

The Old Person Diet

Egg salad sandwich

Tuna salad sandwich

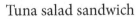

Mixed frozen vegetables

Boiled vegetables

A nice warm glass of buttermilk

Liver and onions

Soup

Unidentifiable mush

CANDY IS DANDY

As you are now an Old Person, your taste buds are not the same taste buds they once were. Those same flavor-receptive bumps that once tasted Salisbury steaks at the finest restaurant in town, sodas that cost a nickel, or the kiss of a thankful Bess Truman at the end of the War have seen their powers dwindle to near-uselessness.

But do not despair, for now you can get close to enjoying the taste of something with the powerful sweetness of individually wrapped peppermint discs, butterscotch discs, and other varieties of hard candy that come in disc form. Also appealing about hard candy to the Old Person is that teeth are not necessarily necessary to enjoy them. Furthermore, they are very economical, as a bag of 300 butterscotch discs costs no more than a dollar, never spoils, and can be displayed in your sitting room for years on end in your finest floral patterned porcelain dish.

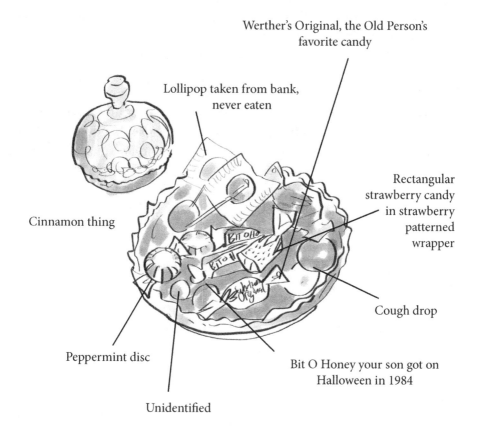

Werther's Original, the Old Person's favorite candy

Lollipop taken from bank, never eaten

Rectangular strawberry candy in strawberry patterned wrapper

Cinnamon thing

Cough drop

Peppermint disc

Bit O Honey your son got on Halloween in 1984

Unidentified

THE OLD PERSON HALL OF FAME: SOUP

Old Persons and Soup just go together. They're two peas in a pod! That reminds us of split-pea soup, which, as it's soft, mushy, bland, and made with a vegetable that hasn't been popular since 1950 — along with ham, a meat considered a holiday-only meat to anyone over the age of 60 — a particular Old Person favorite. Yes, Old Persons and soup are proverbially joined at the rapidly disintegrating hip. They're like Hope and Crosby, or split pea and ham, chicken and rice, or noodles and broth.

The chance that an Old Person *might* come in for a 10 a.m. lunch or 4:30 p.m. supper is the only reason restaurants even have soup on the menu. Nobody under the age of 60 ever eats soup, and those that do are children under the care of a grandparent for a few hours. Old Persons, due to the failing state of their teeth and digestive systems, love soup as they don't have to chew it or actively digest it. It just goes right on through them, and also it's hot and the cheapest thing on the menu, because, as you know, Old Persons are on a fixed income.

Here's to soup, the thing that would be on the Old Person coat of arms, if such a thing were to exist.

CHAPTER FIVE
FASHION SHOW!

You're an Old Person, sure, but are you ready to be a *stylish* Old Person? Read on to find out about all the tried-and-true choices in the world of Old Person clothing, hairstyles, and tenny-runners.

Picking Your Old Person Shoes

Keds. A shoe closely associated with sock hops in the '50s, little kids running lemonade stands in the '70s, and Old Persons forevermore. They're the cheaply made, quick-to-fall-apart, uncomfortable, inexpensive canvas shoes that are the footwear of your life. For an even bigger Old Person kick, skip the name-brand ones for a pair of generics purchased at the local pharmacy or variety store.

Loafers. Your "dress" shoes. The kind you don't have to wear anymore since you retired from the job that made you dress up. Banish these to the back of the closet…except for the couple of hours a week you have to match these up with some khakis and a golf shirt for church.

New Balance. Athletic shoes — what you used to refer to under the inaccurate umbrella term of "tennis shoes" — finally infiltrated Old Person culture recently, in the form of New Balance sneakers. High-cut and boxy, they're at their most natural if paired with white socks pulled all the way up. They're great shoes for puttering about the house or going on a very slow stroll around the neighborhood.

Slippers. Soft, comfortable shoes to wear around the house. You should never go barefoot as an Old Person because you might step on something, and you should never tool around just in socks or stockings because you could slip and fall down the stairs. The solution: slippers. They're soft like socks, very comfortable, and you can wear them outside to go get the mail or the newspaper.

Crocs. Publicly acceptable slippers. Always wear socks underneath.

Insoles. Put these in every pair of shoes you've got. You'd like to shake the hand of the remarkable Dr. Scholl (or maybe his foot! Hahaha, we're just kidding!).

WHICH OLD PERSON HAIRSTYLE IS RIGHT FOR YOU?

You're an Old Person, and you've got to look the part. It's time to select one of the few pre-approved Old Person hairstyles available to you. Each connotes wisdom, life experience, humility, appropriateness, and most importantly, elderlyism. But you've got some freedom of choice here, so pick the one that's most in line with your unique brand of Old Personness.*

*NOTE: For *male* Old Persons. Female Old Persons have only one choice of hairstyles, and that's the one both modeled by and named the "Betty White."

For men:

Closely cropped, bordering on a buzz-cut
If you served in the Armed Forces, thank you for your service. Also, this military-style haircut is the one for you. Not only do you probably still already have it, keeping it all these years, but it's tough, manly, and let's people know you're not some kind of hippie or, God forbid, a namby-pamby pretty boy. Besides, it fits nicely under your Marine Corps or U.S. Army baseball cap, which is the only thing besides that haircut that more explicitly lets people know you have a military background. This is the perfect style for tough old guys who don't want to be messed around or taken any less seriously than they did in their younger years, from which they're having a hard time moving on.

Bald
Have you been struck with the heartbreak of alopecia? It's okay, you're an Old Person now, and not seen as a sexual or virile figure in any way. You can finally just give up and be totally bald. Or, go for the partial bard look and keep those little patches on the sides over the ears. Those make you look hapless and helpless, and people will know that you're totally non-threatening. This is the perfect style for a fun, easy-going grandpa kind of Old Person.

Silver fox
You know the kind: short, parted over, maybe a little mousse or gel thrown in there. Are you a cocky old guy who used to tool around town in your cool convertible, and you still do that on the weekends? Then this is the

haircut for you, you rich, smug, old asshole who always looks like you're on your way to or from a game of golf or berating a member of the service industry. Plus the ladies both young and old will think you look handsome or "distinguished" (which is a French word meaning "old handsome"), just like Merv Griffin, George Hamilton, or even that rebellious young scamp Steve Martin.

A note about hair for men
No matter your choice, you can still have plenty of hair coming out of your nose and ears. After all, you're an Old Person!

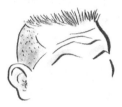

Closely cropped, bordering on a buzz-cut

Bald

Silver Fox

Light Blue Pants

Since at least the rise of polyester as a popular clothing fabric in the 1960s, Old Persons, men primarily, have enjoyed purchasing crisp, clean, slick, tight-about-the-thighs slacks made from the fabric. Invariably, they have been light blue. No one is quite sure why this is; many theories, all of them inconclusive, have bandied about the Oldologist community for years.

Before you were an Old Person, there is no way you would ever allow yourself to be seen in something as tacky as a pair of light blue, shiny pants, with or without pleats. And yet here you are, an Old Person, intrigued with the idea of these unique pants, or as you are wont to call them now, "trousers," or "sansabelts."

It is also unknown where a newly old Old Person goes to purchase these periwinkle pants. Our research at C.O.O.T. has proved fruitless; it is apparently a bit of knowledge that Old Persons pass on only to one another within their community. Perhaps there's a catalog? One study at C.O.O.T. suggested that light blue polyester pants spontaneously appear in the chest of drawers of a man on the eve of his 65th birthday.

Hats Off? Hats On!

How do you top an Old Person? The only way is with a hat, of course! Old Persons adore and appreciate hats. Not only do they keep the sun out of your weak and sensitive eyes, they also hide bald spots and are forever hip and fashionable. You know who wore hats? John F. Kennedy, Eliot Ness, Cary Grant, and the most elegant lady at church, to name just a few enviable individuals. Also, you don't want to catch skin cancer, do you?

But which Old Person hat is right for you? Select from one of these Old Person hat options to complete your Old Person look.

Fisherman hat

Ball cap denoting military service

Old Fart baseball cap

Lady visor, same but with a plastic shield

Golf visor

Bushman cap

Church hat

Floppy gardening hat

MAKE THE CHANGE TO A CHANGE PURSE

It's been ages since anything of value has been priced to a point where it could be paid for solely with coins. Things are just so darn expensive these days, a fact you will certainly notice as an Old Person and also speak of on a regular basis (*see,* **The Old Person Money Philosophy**).

However, you are an Old Person now, and despite the uselessness of coins, it's time that you got rid of your wallet (or the near-Old Person accessory, the money clip) and started carrying a change purse. It's simply what an Old Person does.

Having a change purse allows you to participate in a number of time-honored Old Person activities, such as:

• Offering shiny coins to your grandchildren

• It's a "tip" to Douglas, the nice young man from the Meals on Wheels.

• Complaining about how things are more expensive than they were in the old days.

• Displaying your love of paisley or floral patterns. As the change purse manufacturers cater exclusively to the Old Person, the only available kinds of change purses are paisley or floral prints.

> ## YES WE...CANE!
> NO OLD PERSON IS FULLY DRESSED WITHOUT THEIR CANE. PRETTY MUCH ANY CANE WILL DO THE TRICK OF GIVING YOU SOMETHING TO LEAN ON DURING THE INCREDIBLY STRESSFUL AND PRECARIOUS ACTIVITY OF LIGHT WALKING. BUT WE RECOMMEND THE METAL ONE WITH THE FOUR LITTLE FEET ON IT. IT KIND OF LOOKS LIKE A FRIENDLY ROBOT'S CLAW!

CHAPTER SIX
AROUND THE HOUSE

Sometimes it's nice to hang around the ol' homestead and enjoy it, now that you've got it just the way you want it. Here's how to make your home (and lawn) as Old Person-friendly as possible.

Puttering (or Puttering Around)

Now that you're old, you can also retire, meaning you're finally able to enjoy the fruits of your labors in what was likely a lengthy career with a single company or civil service office. And by that we mean, your house, which is more than likely a split-level home in the suburbs of a medium-sized city with four bedrooms, three bathrooms, and a two-car garage on which you took out a 30-year fixed-rate mortgage which you recently paid off. That house is yours, and you can do whatever you want to that house, of yours.

You always *could* make any improvements or changes to that house of course, but now you've finally got the time, what with work being over, the kids moving out, and you waiting patiently for death. But also, you're a little infirm and unsure on your feet to be climbing up ladders and wielding an electric drill, so instead of actually taking on any major home improvement projects, engage in the next best thing: the tried and true Old Person pastime of puttering.

Puttering technically involves doing stuff around the house, but not *really*. Sure, you might actually fix a shelf or clean the garage, but you probably won't, because that's not really the point of puttering.

Puttering means taking those certain, vaguely problematic boxes out of the attic. Puttering means taking those same boxes and putting them down in the basement. Or you could sift through the contents of those boxes. Or don't. You could putter in the garage and mess around with that boat. Or the motorcycle in there. Or the classic car. Or just look at them admiringly and involve them in some big plans you know you're not going to keep.

At any rate, you're going to be doing this all day, every day, taking breaks only to work on your lawn or landscaping, or critique your also Old Person neighbors' puttering and landscaping habits. And make sure you have the garage door open all day long, to make for good airflow and temperature control while you're puttering. But really it's so everyone can see how you just putter all day, your Old Person "flex," as the kids say.

Your Old Person Living Room

With your newly bestowed status as an Old Person coming down the pike, it's time to do some redecorating. You'll need to get your living room, or sitting room, up to par with Old Person standards, both in appearance and function. With just a few accent pieces and minor style choices, you'll easily have a living room that just screams "Grandma's House 1960" or "Grandma's House 1972" or "Grandma's House 1994."

Television. You don't need one of those fancy flat-screens you hang on the wall. You want such a large purchase to be, well, large — a two-foot thick and five-feet wide television console (with a 24-inch screen) that is essentially a piece of furniture because it's as big as a couch. You can put knick-knacks on top of it!

Stereo. Also called a "hi-fi" or record player, it's not a multi-format stereo at all but a record player with a needle that hasn't been changed ever. After all, you only use it to play Christmas albums at Christmas and occasionally a Mantovani record (*see* **Old Person Music**).

Couch. Get a design that's both alluring and conversation-starting — something floral or paisley. And make sure to protect your investment with a plastic covering.

Recliner. For the gentleman of the home. Notice the well-worn seat.

Ottomans and footstools. The more the better!

TV trays. Set these up by the couch and recliner, and you can eat dinner *while* you watch your programs! So decadent!

Chandelier. What a beautiful light fixture that does not match the rest of the décor whatsoever. Now you're thinking like a traditional Old Person!

On Getting Others Off Your Lawn: An Old Person Call to Action

There's nothing more important to an Old Person than their lawn. That perfectly manicured, artificially geometric patch of carefully and scientifically modified foliage that needs constant watering will remind you how much you love golf, and also how great your suburban house looks. But these neighborhood youngsters, they're seemingly *always* on your lawn. You have to stay constantly vigilant to make sure they stay off that lawn! We suppose they can't help it — your lawn is a very good lawn, and how can they not want to play ball or roughhouse on its lush green surface? But they mustn't! That's *your* lawn, Old Person, and they better heed your constant warning and get off of it! After all, you're the one mowing it at 6 a.m. every Saturday morning without fail!

---

5 Great Ways to Tell Kids to Get Off Your Lawn

1. Open the window, grumble, and shake a fist
2. Stand up from your seat on the porch and shake your cane at them in a threatening manner.
3. Turn the sprinklers on.
4. Call them "delinquents" and hold up the phone receiver while you threaten to call the police.
5. Take whatever ball or Frisbee disc they've got and try to break it while shouting "Bah!"

How to Tell Miscreant Youngsters Who Don't Speak the English to Get Off Your Lawn

Spanish: "Sal de mi cesped"
French: "Descendre ma pelouse"
Vietnamese: "Ra khỏi vườn cỏ của tôi"
Mandarin: "Líkāi wǒ de cǎopíng"
Korean: "Nae madang-eseo naga"

"My Lovely Lawn"
A Poem by Jimmy Stewart
(as recited on *The Tonight Show Starring Johnny Carson***)**

My lovely lawn is lovely
How I love to watch it grow

Its blades are all the same length
Because I cut it just so

It's as lush as it is green
Because I use a fertilizer

To think, I used to just let it grow wild
But I've since grown much wiser

INSIDE AN OLD PERSON'S MEDICINE CABINET

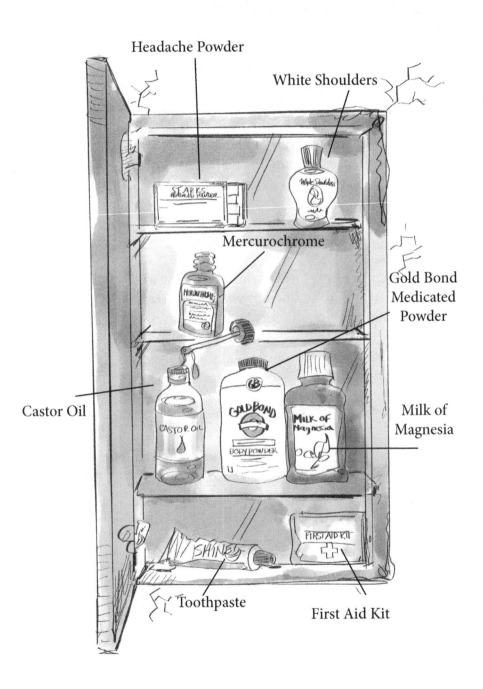

Headache Powder

White Shoulders

Mercurochrome

Gold Bond
Medicated
Powder

Castor Oil

Milk of
Magnesia

Toothpaste

First Aid Kit

COMPANY'S COMING!

What's the most important thing in life? Is it ensuring the happiness and comfort of your spouse and immediate family and, God willing, grandchildren? Or is it making sure that *you* are happy and content in every way?

No. Absolutely not. None of this. It's catering to the every assumed whim of, and impressing via a very old-fashioned and well-established set of standards, company. Yes, company is coming. Who is company? Anybody from your adult children to friends from church, former work associates, or distant relatives, or that neighbor who moved away to Phoenix about 10 years ago and is back in town this weekend for a funeral. That's "company," and we must project upon them our anxieties and the notion that they have very lofty demands.

Now is the time to bring out the extra spare set of everything, the stuff so nice that you are only to use it rarely and sparingly. The extra-fluffy white towels? Those are for company. The high-thread count sheets just waiting on the untouched bed in the guest room? That's all for company, and nobody but company.

Don't even think about dining on those china plates with roses on them, or busting out your wedding silver. No special occasion is special enough, except for when people you sort of know and sort of like are coming over for a single meal or to spend one night. You must impress them, and your reputation must precede you as an Old Person who has Very Nice Things. Those plates and silver will come to extra good use when you bring out dessert, which you never have ordinarily, and that dessert is a frozen cheesecake that's been in the freezer since before your neighbor moved to Phoenix.

Chapter Seven
That's Entertainment!

No, we're not talking about the greatest documentary ever made, the one that's just a collection of clips of grand old musicals. This chapter is all about the arts, culture, and diversions just waiting for you, Old Person.

The Printed Word

In that great big world out there that's so complicated and scary, who can an Old Person trust? Certainly your minister, mayor, pharmacist, TV weatherman, and insurance agent, but other than that, what amorphous, non-living concepts can be counted on to deliver truthful, helpful, and, it should go without saying, totally unbiased information?

Typeset words on a printed page.

If it's in print, it must be true and it *is* true. This is a belief of Old Persons, although it's also just a fact. "They" just wouldn't be allowed to print something if it wasn't true. Publishing something makes a statement official and real. It's just the way it is.

In practice, you can trust a book but not that internet. They can change that whenever they like on the computer! But a book? A book is done. It's finished. It's printed. It's written in stone! (Or paper, which is made out of wood, which is kind of like a stone.)

A catalog can't steal your credit card number and give it to the bad guys like an on-line-internet-web-site does and will do. That's why Old Persons buy all of their clothes, novelty items, and gifts through catalogs that are randomly sent to them in the mail.

Of course, the daily newspaper is the ultimate in trustable print media. They've got reporters out there on the beat, getting scoops, telling it like it is. And they also run all those fun wire reports and lifestyle interest articles. There's literally no way of forwarding an article on the internet (unless it's a very alarming email forward, or a list of emailed jokes about how it is amusing to be an Old Person). With a newspaper, you can clip out articles and mail them to your adult children. They'll get a kick out of it!

The newspaper is also a source of an Old Person's favorite topic: the weather. It shows you what somebody 16 hours prior thought the weather was going to be today, as well as the weather in various other places around the state. Where your adult children live. It's so interesting!

They've also got the TV listings in there, so you can plan out what you want to watch and make sure to be home in time.

And don't forget the Sunday supplement, *Parade Magazine*. It's the Old Person's best source of lifestyle information outside of the AARP magazine, which is *free* (with membership) and as a printed source is also steadfast and true.

The glory of print media is why you're right to wait for the mail and its glorious arrival every day, which may contain in it the greatest magazine in the history of the world for the Old Person — *Reader's Digest*.

And you can't look at a map on your phone, nor a picture of your grandkid. You've got to print those out and, as for the latter, frame or laminate it.

Yes, all print media is to be believed and all information on a screen is to be dismissed. Unless, of course, it's some deeply troubling, unsourced, sensationalistic information that pops up on the cable news screen or on your Facebook feed. Then *that* is true, and supersedes all other printed information.

Cozy Up with a Good Book

With old age and retirement, you've got all the time in the world to read to your heart's content. You can finally read all the great works, or those books you've bought that are just on your shelves shamefully untouched because life got in the way.

Unfortunately, you're not allowed to read any of those. You're an Old Person, and you've got to read your Old Person books, and *only* your Old Person books. But take comfort and pride in the knowledge that you're now part of the vast swaths of Old Persons whose collective tastes keep the publishing industry afloat. Nobody *really* buys Pulitzer Prize-winning novels; they buy smug and smarmy political hand-wringing screeds from conservative cable news personalities. Their target audience, on print and on screen: Old Persons like you.

But those are just the urgent reads. As an Old Person, you've got to give yourself a constant diet of Old Person reading materials, and that is strictly divided along gender lines. Female Old Persons will not be able to get enough of crime and murder mystery novels, enjoying looking on and judging as foolish fictional people get married and brave and smart men and women catch their killers. Old Persons especially enjoy the novels where an Old Person solves mysteries when they aren't running a bakery, being a busybody neighbor, or writing mystery novels.

Hero Old Person TV Sleuth mystery author Jessica Fletcher

Male Old Persons, however, get to read about big exciting things done by the men that they wish they could've been. They, and now you, like to read very large nonfiction books about men who are cowboys, men who command submarines, and men who are Winston Churchill, Abraham Lincoln, or Teddy Roosevelt.

O.P.T.V. (Old Person Television)

Your tastes in television have changed very drastically and specifically now that you're an Old Person. First, get rid of all those newfangled Apple Boxes and web streaming deely-bobbers. Broadcast TV, coming into your house over an antenna, is just fine, nothing fancy, and just what you need. The networks air nice programs with nothing offensive that gently entertain and rarely rile up the blood. (Except for when the news tells you what bad things it says are happening. Such a shame!)

Here's a grid you can cut out and tape up next to the TV so you can remember which programs you like and when they're on!

Middays

My Three Sons reruns

Perry Mason reruns

Bonanza reruns

Your stories

Every weekday:

6:00 pm: Local news

7:00 p.m. *Jeopardy!*

7:30 p.m. *Wheel of Fortune*

Monday evening: *Dancing With the Stars*

Tuesday evening: CBS crime shows

Wednesday evening: CBS crime shows

Thursday evening: CBS crime shows

Friday evening: CBS crime shows

Saturday evening: *Lawrence Welk* reruns

Sunday evening: *60 Minutes*

The Old Person Hall of Fame: Mama from Mama's Family

With the exception of *Matlock*, there have been few television programs expressly aimed at an audience made up entirely of Old Persons, not since that cursed day when the broadcasters switched from glorious black-and-white to vulgar color. The best and only other newer show for the Old Person that is also about an Old Person — and a shamelessly ideal Old Person at that — is *Mama's Family*.

It's a show about old-fashioned values, old-fashioned people, living an old-fashioned life in an old-fashioned town. When it first aired 40 years ago, it already felt like it was 40 years old. Also, and to the delight of Old Persons both then and now, it was on nice and early, about 6:30 p.m., making for a nice Saturday night treat that you didn't have to stay up late to watch and then be groggy for church the next morning.

But what makes *Mama's Family* an all-time old-timer's delight is its main character, Thelma Harper. Played by Vicki Lawrence, a veteran of '70s TV variety shows (loved by all Old Persons), Thelma Harper is both a parody of an Old Person and the embodiment of the Old Person. She's grumpy, angry, stubborn, and uncooperative — everything an Old Person is or strives to be. She doesn't take any guff, has a suitably Old Person name (Thelma), and doesn't take any guff from her ne'er-do-well adult children, who she deftly avoids blame for raising into crummy adults. She's the very picture of old, too, with her shapeless floral dresses, support hose, orthopedic shoes, permanent-style hair, and giant glasses. She looks like the iconic Old Person that she truly is.

Old Person Music

Music is lovely and one of the best things about being alive. However, as far as an Old Person is concerned, it should never be used to express overwhelming feelings that may agitate, upset, or rile up a person in any way. Music should not excite — it should *calm*. That's why they play music at the pharmacy and the grocery store — nice, soft, and gentle music to keep you feeling fine when you're running errands.

Similarly, music is there to remind you of The Good Old Days, like World War II, or the Korean War. As an Old Person, you are no longer allowed to like any of that newfangled rock and roll or, God forbid, that rap nonsense (which they should put a "c" on the front of — isn't that fiendishly clever?). Sorry, but your tastes run strictly from the WWII era through to just before Elvis and the Beatles arrived and ruined everything. Big band is the only band you need, and as far as singers go, they just don't make them any better than they did Bing Crosby, Patti Page, and Frank Sinatra (but even he's only suitable for setting a mood when it's time to "make whoopee" or "have marital relations").

Also acceptable is church music, but *not* gospel. The Lord must know you love him by singing bland, mid-tempo, half-hearted songs of vague praise. And that's all the excitement you can handle, bub!

About the only time when jaunty music is permissible is when you're watching an old Hollywood movie musical comedy, or seeing one live down at the community theater. You'll be whistling those tunes for weeks!

THE OLD BALL GAME

Well, if you aren't a very lucky Old Person! You're in for a big treat today, because it's a beautiful day and you're headed down to the ballpark to see a ballgame!

In Old Person vernacular, anytime "ball" is used as a prefix — in front of "park," "game," or "player," for example — it indicates a discussion of baseball, the only sport Old Persons care about or will even acknowledge the existence of. As such, Old Persons are the only people who still care about baseball, as it is crucial to the Old Person experience. Not only is it conservative to the point of square, traditional to the point of hopelessly dated, and completely and wonderfully boring, it's also about as slow-moving as a thing technically considered a sport can be. Baseball is the "National Pastime," but only for Old Persons, and only as it pertains to watching it.

Baseball is a remarkably robust conduit for reminiscence and nostalgia. The framework of the game is built upon a foundation of concepts like "the golden years" and "the way things used to be sure were better," viewed through a black-and-white lens tinted by childhood memories. That point of view sublimates all the negative and racist implications of loving baseball, good old-fashioned baseball. As you ramble on about how "it used to be better" and how "they sure don't make 'em like they used to" in regards to the likes of "Joltin'" Joe DiMaggio and Stan "The Man" Musial, you can go on and on and just only imply vaguely that you're glorifying a time when there were few or not any players of color to muck up this gentlemanly sport. (*We used to wear suits and hats to the games! Why don't we do that anymore?* You will wonder aloud.)

THE OLD PERSON ALL-TIME BASEBALL GREATS SQUAD

HAT BAKER
HANK BANKER
CHAP MILLER
HURRICANE JOHANNSEN
TWO-FINGER BLACK
ONE-FINGER BROWN
NO HANDS CHARNLETON
KIK KIPPLINGTON
SILAS SILASMAN

You'll delight in the Seventh Inning Stretch. Not only will you relish the chance to get up and stretch your legs, because you've been sitting in a cramped seat for two hours already watching men sort of maybe run around a square and play catch, but as an Old Person, you love the sing-along to "Take Me Out to the Ballgame," the only time you'll sing outside of church. But then, a ballpark is kind of like the great American church, so sing that old standard with patriotic pride bordering on religious fervor not seen since before the game, when you solemnly held your hand on your heart and removed your cap for "The Star-Spangled Banner."

During a game, you'll also likely fancy the idea of traveling to every Major League ballpark before you die but will dismiss the notion when you remember that they tore down the old Polo Grounds and Ebbets Field after they shipped off all those teams to kooky California.

Grab yourself some old-timey snacks like Cracker Jack, and also a hot dog, except you call them "frankfurters" or "Coney Dogs" or some other long disused or narrowly regional distinction.

Are you going to keep score in that arcane way? Of course you are. You're an Old Person, and it's "a tradition" to do that.

The smell of the grass, the sound of the organ, the bark of the vendors — yes, it's a lovely day to witness live in person eight total minutes of professional sports action spread out over the course of three and a half hours.

THE GLAMOROUS WORLD OF MOVIE STARS!

These celebrities that are famous these days, the ones from all those reality shows and MTV music videos and loud situation comedies that aren't geared toward someone of your age or impeccable taste, the ones that came up after you were young, or who are stars of entire media formats that you don't even understand? They've all got no talent, not like the old stars, who were really something. Part of being an Old Person is worshipping those legendary (meaning they're long done) stars of the Silver Screen and the Golden Age while simultaneously deriding the similar devotion to presently alive stars by today's younger people.

It's up to you to keep the memory of the old-time celebrities alive. Discuss them with other Old Persons. Point them out when they're on an old movie on the TV. Let someone in earshot know when someone who isn't them shows up on the TV but sort of reminds you of them, and then go off on how they don't make movie stars like they used to.

Also informing your blind worship of celebrities of yore is that you, as a regular Old Person, will have met a celebrity one time, many years ago, likely on an airplane or in an elevator during your one trip to The Big City. Talk about this encounter constantly. If it's a vaguely remembered celebrity, that's all the better. Constantly regale others with the story of that time you met "Dandy" Don Meredith or a cast member of *Bonanza*.

As for the rest of your knowledge of celebrity garnered from a lifetime of watching picture shows and network television, you will promptly forget all of this as an Old Person. Oldologists say that the first aspect of memory loss suffered by Old Persons is forgetting the names of every movie and TV star they've ever seen, and once knew. This will lead to the popular Old Person game, however, of "Who Is That and What Have I Seen Them In?"

THE OLD PERSON HALL OF FAME: THE GUY FROM 'ON GOLDEN POND'

The modern idea of the Old Person began in earnest with Henry Fonda's portrayal of Norman Thayer, Jr., in the 1981 Academy Award winning family melodrama *On Golden Pond*. He is everything an Old Person is and ought to be. To whit:

• He fishes.
• He wears a fisherman's hat
• He's not concerned with domestic issues like "relationships" or "being nice to his family."
• He doesn't give a hoot what anybody thinks.
• He's simultaneously both grumpy *and* crotchety.
• He performatively pretends to be sick to death of his wife, as she does for him. All Old Person couples do this, and they're just imitating *On Golden Pond*'s dynamic.
• He's got the best Old Person nickname ever: "Old Poop." It shows that he's old and is just a little offensive and evocative of the bodily functions that Old Persons can't control, but *really* shows that he's a party pooper. Because as an Old Person, it's your right to ruin the fun for everyone. Like an old poop.

Plus, Norman Thayer, Jr. is portrayed by a *real* movie star, Henry Fonda, an actor from the days when a movie star was a movie star! And he won an Oscar for it just before he died, showing that Old Persons do have worth and value and can do things even as they're obviously knocking on death's door.

Bingo!

Congratulations! You've finished *So You Want to Be an Old Person*, which means you're well prepared with a strong body of knowledge. As a special reward, here's a free Bingo card, a guaranteed winner at your next game of Bingo down at the Bingo hall *or* the senior center. Aces!

B	I	N	G	O
1	16	31	46	65
5	17	33	47	64
3	18	FREE	49	63
4	19	34	48	62
2	20	35	50	61

Acknowledgments

The author wishes to express his gratitude to Humorist Books editor Andy Newton and publisher Marty Dundics, who utilized their exemplary comedic taste, creative empathy, and unfailing professionalism to develop this book from an amorphous nugget into exactly the book the author intended for it to be, even before the author knew just what that meant. The author also offers his limitless thanks to Megan, forever patient and with astute constructive criticism on offer, and to Brendan, who tells me what is and what is not funny.

About the Author

Brian Boone has written comedy all over the internet, with his work appearing on *Weekly Humorist*, Someecards, *ClickHole*, *Bunny Ears*, *McSweeney's Internet Tendency*, and *Vulture*. He is also the author of many joke books for children, trivia books for adults, and the novel *Great Men of Science*. Find him on Twitter: @brianbooone.

Oopsies Remember Notes
Use these back pages to jot down important reminders like where you put the remote, & who your current enemies are and why.

Oopsies Remember Notes

Oopsies Remember Notes

Oopsies Remember Notes

OOPSIES REMEMBER NOTES

Oopsies Remember Notes

Oopsies Remember Notes

Oopsies Remember Notes

Made in the USA
Las Vegas, NV
05 December 2023

82174583R00056